ALSO BY DANIELLE PAFUNDA

Pretty Young Thing (Soft Skull, 2005)
My Zorba (Bloof, 2008)
Iatrogenic: Their Testimonies (Noemi, 2010)
Manhater (Dusie, 2012)
Natural History Rape Museum (Bloof, 2013)

THE DEAD GIRLS SPEAK IN UNISON

Danielle Pafunda

The Dead Girls Speak in Unison
© 2017 Danielle Pafunda
Second Edition

Design & composition: Shanna Compton, shannacompton.com
Cover photo: Paula Jane Mendoza
Proofreading for first edition: Monroe Hammond

Published by Bloof Books
PO Box 326
Lambertville NJ 08530
www.bloofbooks.com

Member of CLMP

Bloof Books are printed in the USA by Bookmobile and Spencer Printing. Booksellers, libraries, and other institutions may order direct from us by contacting sales@bloofbooks.com. POD copies are distributed via Ingram, Baker & Taylor, and other wholesalers. Individuals may purchase our books direct from our website, from online retailers such as Amazon.com, or request them from their favorite bookstores.

Please support your local independent bookseller whenever possible.

ISBN-13: 978-0-9965868-6-3
ISBN-10: 0-9965868-6-5

1. American poetry—21st century. 2. Poets, American—21st century.
∞ This paper meets the requirements of ANSI/NISO Z39.48-1992

CONTENTS

- 9 On the front page
- 10 We'll tell you
- 12 Hush, hush. Out the window
- 13 We have been crammed full
- 14 One of us said
- 15 Woe betide us
- 17 The surface world too bright now
- 18 We can't bear.
- 19 *I felt a funeral*, we whisper.
- 21 Though our sticks are split
- 22 Fold yourself over.
- 23 We're ever so tired of sleeping.
- 24 *At the crude nest of the mouth*
- 25 You already knew we were thieves.
- 26 Or robbers, if you insist.
- 27 We can recall in great detail
- 28 Supine, we roll our eyes back
- 29 We have a response
- 30 We used to do it, too.
- 31 Fine. Another trance upon us, then.
- 33 Or lullaby and goodnight.
- 35 We are as ineffective now as we were in life.
- 36 Or else, we are right behind you.
- 37 Our maggots more charming
- 38 We are never alone.
- 41 Don't ask us what it's like

42	Where do you keep your trick
43	Then, we lay back on limestone
44	Trouble
45	Who didn't we love?
47	Radishes sprout through the walls
48	In front of the lake house
49	Who would we be with our teeth
50	It's happy death day.
51	If you're looking for something pretty
53	We are going
55	Hush, now.
56	We came this way. We carved it thus.
57	Where's our deady daddy?
59	Spider-legged leader
60	Time runs short
61	We're so glum.
62	Let us be clear
65	We haven't made any progress.
67	Whatever will you do
68	Positioned neatly
69	One of us has a fright wig.
71	We're weary
73	We aren't much uglier
76	Fuck your circadian rhythm, then.
78	Do not pretend
80	Acknowledgments
81	About the Author

On the front page
life has smeared.

We get no news
of home down here.

No before, no news of storms.
No new noise, no newsy skin
on the surface of things.

We get nothing but the center
of each *o* eaten by a worm
relinquished by a worm

traveling the country
by way of worm, our sorry conduit

our sleaze and scrap nostalgia.

THE CHORUS

We'll tell you
what a corpse is.

It's a girl

with her shoes
on backward.

It's a double-
jointed girl.

It's a glass eye
in a glass jar
in the jaw
of an alligator, girl.

It's a doll

whose eyes move

of their own accord

when you turn
just so.

It's a hollowed-
loop pearl
through which
the worm
can thread
her lonely
troubles.

Her lover
done gone.

1

Hush, hush. Out the window
though it's May, the sleet
comes stinging through.

A bird is struck and limps
on one infested wing.
I am a metropolis, weeps the bird.

As were each of us
with our teeming.
We were worth absolute millions.

A fire, and a world apiece.

And in that world
a blade of grass
stuck in the throat.

And on her ruffled coat
she spat.

2

We have been crammed full
of your unwholesome piggeldy.

Today's lesson
a lesson in stripping.

First you apply the glue
then you scrape the glue
and with the glue
goes your grief.

Tra-la
tra-la.

In the dander is your grief.

In the grit is your grief.

In the aching margins
of your failed relationship
is your grief
and your wrench.
But you know what is lacking?

Of course you do.
We are lacking in you.

CHANT

One of us said

[muffled]

One of us said

[gagging]

One of us said

[a knocking sound]

she'd pull off your face

and mail it to fuck town.

[titters]

CHANT

Woe betide us
woe betide.

Be tied to us.
Some to the post
some by lasso.

Some with one wrist
bound to the other
and both to the ankle

strung

invert

pissing.

Which is a relief
because there are pins
in the gums, and pins

under the nails.
Pins in the scalp
under the thick.

Tied.

Though some of us
were only ever
tied to the hem.

Quaking, or notnumb.
A sort of motion sickness
as when lashed to the mast.

Everything slipped into centrifuge

and always our teeth ached
to sink in, to tear out

with a resounding snap.
The rope frayed
the silk cord threat.

4

The surface world too bright now
wasn't made for spooks like us.
We were made its ridiculed.

Its loose-toothed tenants, late
with rent, tense against a rack
displaying our fine cuts—

a thousand gluey rhinestones
spilling onto a very predictable
warehouse floor. Yawnsome ravage.

The surface world, with oil stains,
pockmarks, flecked metals. Its herds
of endothermic legs and skeletal pollens.

Its multiply coded salts, its loams
of night, *like meat veins in a white urn*
all of which you cannot.

CHANT

We can't bear.

Your chatter.

Any longer.

When you say *no*, we say *now*
when you say *sorry*, we say *sack*.

Hey hey.

Ho ho.

5

I felt a funeral, we whisper.
A shiver as the procession
marches cross our graves.

Such grave robbers
we take the spunk
out of the cemetery

and the blush off the urn.

Take heart, and boil it clean
like a beet. A grief of baby mice.

Under our nails flesh.
Vicious viscous pink
a rivulet runs to the elbow.

Everything tastes dirt
in the companionable ground
where we lie open-mouthed.

And *dirt* means nothing,
just like *day* used to do.
Or *life*.

When it wasn't something
you could get a speck of it
on you.

Stop.

We sound almost chipper
this flock of dun-colored birds.
Broken-beaked maracas.

6

Though our sticks are split
we still get eventide
still get lit, night-capped.

Kidnapped, feet wrapped
in the loopy intestine
of your funny little dream.

You think you've found
the sweetest hole—
to bury your craggy face.

The underworld is burning.
Whatevs, little legs.
Make with the running.

Up the sheets like a ladder
each chanteuse gone to heck
will beckon your wreck.

7

Fold yourself over.
Put this stick in your stick slot.
Oh, beanpoled crater face.

Kill it. Kill it, your darling
downriver.

Your pornographic heart, John Henry,
swelling the top of your long johns
puffing, puffed and filling your kerchief.

Your beeline for the border, the state line.
Let's go waltzing, a'crossing
with a thirteen-year-old

redhead in the hatchback
in the way back
the trunk-like interior

face down, hemorrhaging fear
and that fear mixing with gasoline
to make—

a baby.

8

We're ever so tired of sleeping.
We fail the end of each soggy hour
in this immense bed, stained

with beetle prints and excrement
reminding us that this too
is the world.

Our failures tremor, today
tender at length we failed.
Which is why the vision

of a live nude girl came upon us.
She scalded, she stank up our room.
We yelled, *fuck you to death*

but there she stood
with wiry hairs
shooting out her waxen skin.

Turgid, slumped. Forgiveless.
We won't try to burn her again.
What a failure!

Oh, can you see your house from here?

9

At the crude nest of the mouth
eggs have been
eggs have red run
eggs spilling bright damsel
flies or the crisp roe—

sediment, mineral
disunion

the albumen zombie

the shell and its wake.

FRAGMENT

You already knew we were thieves.

FRAGMENT

Or robbers, if you insist.

10

We can recall in great detail
the startled thread of skin
pulled to reveal the pathogen chasm.

What we once went squeamish
ewwwwing from, it turns out
composes us.

Turned on our spindle, greasy thread
weaves the world's pulsing pain fabric.
Mutton smell, deteriorating harbor,

whole flesh-filled fishy spectacle
itching away in the corner.
We recall the moment

when the knee exploded
the curse of bone-black bled
a name scrawled in ash

on the adulterous hide.
Mother, what mutton.
What kneeling has done.

11

Supine, we roll our eyes back
like the doll's, and *the night
is a starry dome.* The tarry

nightlike inner crust
of earth, and the stars
each one a salty maggot.

A murder of ghosts appears
on the hemlock; it's extra deathy
but don't be stupid, human cylinder.

There is no near to death.
There is only yes
or not   yet.

12

We have a response
to each of your tiresome strangles.
We do clench your face

where our fists used to be.
We do yank your hair
and out so pops a stony gut.

One by one, a popping corn.
You contend each numbered girl
calls up her gunk-crammed cavity.

And you are correct.
That is the shame of living.

13

We used to do it, too.
Put finger to planchet and hope
for something even sluttier

to reveal its shuddering self
on the rod, skittering.
We used to yes or no it.

As though it wouldn't make us blind.

Whose brother is that?
Spying through glass?

Whose punishment is coming?

Bloody Mary. Bloody
her frigid face.
Whose corpsey brother

all wig and claw
and rigid jaw, floating,
bloated, copping a feel?

14

Fine. Another trance upon us, then.
A plague of trances. We are so very
very mystical! We are ever so very

fabric of dark matter
and putrid gash
leaking the scrabble

of legs and every stair
from the bottom up
counted so loudly aloud.

On the first step.
Because we aren't afraid of you
nor of losing you now

for whatever that's worth.

Oh but once upon a time
we could see flesh
and you coming in it

with your rough club, your bear cub,
your chest beat to shreds
and a stain spread on your collar

leach down the aisle, down the well
under the bridge
where all your brides swell.

15

Or lullaby and goodnight.
The fate of a nation
spread on your lap

flammable, stinking
shoe polish
fish or fecal.

A hard slab of butter
cold in her cold mouth
the milk curdled

someone's mummy doll
with her head cracked
and one glass eye jangling.

Another mildewed leather
the rotten pages
of your rotten romance

the rotten clasp
the velvet harboring
a furred-over egg sac.

What can we tell you
that all of those spiders
haven't already spelled out

across your stunned,
still, silent, flesh?
Get. Out. Now.

FRAGMENT

We are as ineffective now as we were in life.

FRAGMENT

Or else, we are right behind you.

FRAGMENT

Our maggots more charming
than any of your statesmen.

16

We are never alone.

We were never alone.

Your star-shaped noses
flowered, your wormy digits
skimmed our wet hems.

Your cars gaping, vomiting
or swallowing us whole.
We couldn't take a breath

without your hair tonic
rushing to fill our lungs
your scabby exhalations

boiled egg, coffee, scab.
Wherever we went on land
we heard that scab

of your dirt clod feet.
Your toenails hooked, ashen heels
scuffing the bedsheets

tearing the bedsheets
to ribbons
selling the ribbons

from your cart
for our last dropped dime
our parents

parched and starved
and scabbed over
while we tied ribbons

and from the window
jumped or pushed
tumbling head over bottom.

And when we burst
into a fountain of coins.
Or else a lark song. Or there

a poisoned ivy bloomed
an anthill thick with blister
blossomed, or nature's scab itself

pissed a thin trickle.
The city came with bleach.
The city came with children

hopscotching, with ice creams.
No shadow dogging you
your mother in the ground tossing.

A pint of spittle, and still
there's a sizable rat in your throat.

17

Don't ask us what it's like
in that moment when the body
skitters away from that stupid

sheepy shape of breath.
Down here, no one asks.
We all died

boot to throat.
We all went out
shrieking some bloody name.

Our tongues swelled
you kissed
our numb fingers.

It was all very touching.
The creak of your sob
in your irredeemable face

your wooden gait
on the frosty hillside.
No one axe.

No one chitters—

18

Where do you keep your trick
now that we're so buried dead
and our teeth like pearls

strung round our powdered necks
above, then below our gashes?

An animal sleeps in your bed.
Like a person, its head
oozing on the pillow

and its hindquarters
crushed into the mattress.
We could go on.

Your car is full of trash.
Your face
is full of trash

your trash the trashiest
for blocks around.
A receipt for turpentine

wiggles out of your wallet
and out of your mouth
the turpentine spills.

19

Then, we lay back on limestone
in sodden undies and counted
the scorpion stars.

And when they fell
into our open guts
our torsos spread like brides.

Get into our limbic chambers!

One day you will punch
the wrong grouse in the gut
and her stingers pour

over your guilt, your quilt
your skin
your hot little grin.

FRAGMENT

    Trouble

    hobble-tied.

20

Who didn't we love?

With an arm
loose out the window
suddenly rent and arterial.

In the baby's crib
one white
kitten heel

shrieking.

On the hooked rug
two daisies
crusted over.

The pinstripe
and rosette paper
streaming with it.

In one glossy ringlet
a ribbon of bees
a ribbon of spittle

a ribbon of promises

not to

ever.

In one glassed eye
bloodshot
a gnat.

Who didn't we take up with?

Who wasn't holding
a very pretty
bang in a sack?

21

Radishes sprout through the walls
their hairy roots, wire recordings
transmitters, the dead's radio

radio death. We stir in our sleep.
Millipedes cross themselves.
Who's weeping for her child?

Better buried with his mother
than hauling himself up
into the maw of his own trou.

The tip of whose tongue
teases your name?

We'll come for you.
And in your domicile
we'll plant our hooks

and in your eyes
we'll hook our beaks.

22

In front of the lake house
someone has drowned
and drowned again

and even his bones have sunk
and drowned.

It is all in the ugly past
where bones made soup
and soup made do

and everyone bedded down
a weak and feral bed.

A special disease
makes sponge of your skeleton.

Soak up the lake water
soak up the muck.

It's all the same to us.

FRAGMENT

Who would we be with our teeth

all shattered by buckshot

the beetle's-back veil?

HYMN

It's happy death day.

It's the day on which
every dead thing
becomes a girl.

Most of us were girls
in life, but all of us
are dead girls.

We have
that certain girlish gait.
We have pains in our nethers

and pins in our pinworms
and wheels of licorice
wheeling away, whirling, oh!

23

If you're looking for something pretty
nestled in the fold
of this leprous bosom

come closer. Snap, snap.

We loved craftily. We infected
ourselves, and tranq'd ourselves
and drank ourselves silly and sang:

> *Oh! What a dumb-dumb-*
> *ugly-duck, a useless piece*
> *of blooded meat.*

Then in the dark beneath
musty woolens bunched
snuggled and fed

a slinky heaven.

And now?

And now?

Nothing soft slinks our way
that isn't wet
with what you'd call

carrion or currency.

24

We are going
to give you
the big C.

We are going to
knock it around
in the plastic water pitcher

and pour you a glass.
A hair embedded in an ice cube.
A tooth embedded in an ice cube.

When you were a small child
with small hands and feet
you made stupid wishes

and now we are here to grant them.

Down here
we have a room
full of your bleats

which are still very boring.
You must have the big C.
You look uncomfortable.

You have a hook
in your gait
a crook in your cavalry.

You don't know where to turn
so follow this arrow

and we'll take you in.

25

Hush, now.

In a house like ours
stay quiet.
Keep moist

or your skin will split
and spill your secrets
across the carpet

one stupid bagworm
after another.

Hush. Do not disturb
our needles
squalling thread.

We're stitching up
all your fancy mistakes.

We're stitching up
your mother's face.

We're going to stitch you a new one.

We're going to take our time.

FRAGMENT

We came this way. We carved it thus.
That was our crack and plank.

26

Where's our deady daddy?
Where's our dear dead
dada man?

We're all dolled up.
We're curls and pearls
and ruffled pants.

We've tacked our skin
back onto bones, and hissing
roaches at our throats.

Gemless, rigged.
We're daddy's girls
we're apples

pierced through
the heart, the socket
where the heart

or the eye once was.
We've his eyes, in fact
his expression fixed

a fix, a needle
dropping down
a syringe full of seed

straight into the cavity
of this bombed-out hide.

FRAGMENT

Spider-legged leader
of that fey
and itsy nation

is it really a new year?

The clock has a hitch
and the wedding walks.

27

Time runs short
each regrettable dawn.
We drop back

on the mildewed mattress.
Who's to say it's any worse
down here

than it was above
when we had silk
soaked in ether

jammed deep into
our scullery holes?
Who's to say

that a skull
full of onyx hurts
any more or less

than that greedy shiv,
that salty rub
crying out

our ropey dugs?

LULLABY

We're so glum.
We've nothing left
but each other's pity.

The bed's flooded.
One of us floats on her back
sockets weeping salt

the husk of her tongue
hissing that same ballad.

> *My rosy bab, my sugar pup,*
> *a boot in the barley,*
> *her skull in the clover.*

The bed leaches, a breech.

28

Let us be clear
about the devil baby.
We loved him.

He was our only love.

We were
only happy
one time.

With him
trailing blood
ectoplasm

desperate for food.

Half-blind, shrieking
his glassy nails
sunk deep in our dugs.

We loved his
Stygimoloch breath
the prehistoric way

he gutted a fish.

We ran tablets of sulfur
over his skin

to quell the blisters.

We weren't cowering.

If you beat your wife
if your wife looks upon
an image of goats

if your wife
rolls in the arms
of another wife.

If your wife is vain
if she has a tail of her own
if she has a sister with horns

if her father rent her out
if her uncles clutter her basin
if she hold a doll aloft alive

and wear her hair in three braids
and sing
with slickened tongue.

And when he was born
and you first split his skull
in his mother's arm

and then his mother's skull
on the eiderdown
and then the bed

down its cursed middle.
And when you wept
and began again

with a pale little rabid
just sprung from school.

29

We haven't made any progress.

When the auditor comes for us
we'll hold out our hands
full of fly casings, pollen spurs.

We've had nothing to eat
but our own hair
for the last dozens of years.

We're strung in the gut
catgutted, glutted.
We smell of mutton.

Plaintive, you want a chance
to hold one of us
to your throb-sick chest.

You want to freeze
and to plow your face
deep into her coffin.

And in there, a world.

You think you can live
harnessed
to her decaying nightdress

you think you can live
on hair and rue?

Then here is our welcome mat
woven from the wig
of your maiden voyage.

30

Whatever will you do
now that your fins have burst
and your heart grown fat?

Your heart hobbled
slogging in its sack of fats
its membrane webbed over

with a lovelorn scum.
In your pelt, you find lice
and they spell out her name.

Who do you know
who trembles against
a pane of wintered glass?

Little sparrow, sweet mint?

A sucker for a silken bladder
a sucker for such perks.

31

Positioned neatly
on the concrete slab
in the perfect yawn

of porch light
a wishbone.

It could be hers.

Though it's a cat's.

It could be the last letter
you ever receive.

FABLE

One of us has a fright wig.
She slaps it on to tell the story.

> *A monster opened her legs*
> *and spat the girl into the world.*
>
> *A terrible monster, spread wide.*
> *She held the girl's head*
> *underwater for forty days.*
>
> *And when that girl would not drown,*
> *she held her head in dirt*
> *for forty more.*
>
> *With a mouthful of beetles*
> *and leavings, the girl wept—*
> *"Mumma!"*
>
> *A monster, she pushed the girl*
> *deeper down and gorged herself*
> *on red fruit and red wine.*
>
> *She sneezed.*
> *She sobbed*
> *when men touched her.*
> *And when men*

*no longer touched her.
She hated the girl
to ribbons.*

*And then the girl
returned and said,
"You are a pig, Mumma."*

But the girl was only oinking,
and mother already dead.

32

We're weary
of our lessons.
Here we sit

motherless calves.
Here we stitch
and squirm

with worms for laces
and the drone of bees
in our otherwise hollow

holes.
Lowing, languid
rowing the cesspool

with broad-brimmed hats
our harpies
and catgut parasols.

We're tired of transcribing.
We're tired of meting out
the meat-life dirge

of trying to keep
your hands off the girls.

Suck one, we say.

Suck one hard
and bite your tongue.

33

We aren't much uglier
in death
than we were in life.

We each had a mustache,
fat thighs, speckled skin,
cold sores, pitted pores.

Hair on our knuckles,
our toes, which were all broken
and our knees also fatted.

Our asses flattened, but wide,
whatever
however positioned.

We were ugly.
We had pores and fungus.
We had protists

we were made
entirely
out of bacteria.

We wore our hair up
and our scalps retched.
Blood-streaked fluid

from pinprick scabs
scratched open,
clotted skin, clotted breath,

we stank.

Our food
never digested properly.

Bags of meat lodged
in our innermost quarters
former lives, rotting there.

We were exhausted
crowded with meat.
We held up our arms

and our veins rang out
through the cellulite
through layer after layer

of dead cells and staph.

Our skulls were moist
soft as a frog's

barely preserved.

Our lips, parched, cracked.
Our nails split
as though along a seam.

A shiny web of busted skin
on each muggy breast.

You see why it was easy.

We had cankles
we never loved you.

34

Fuck your circadian rhythm, then.
We keep queer time,

bolt time, we keep time
against a ticking
egg sac.

We keep the hands going
in the most
inappropriate tic.

We scale the wall
in a wee hour
and piss all over your lilacs.

We mix cat vomit and quinine.

Fuck your lulla lulla lullaby
your twee lanterns

and the cheap rust chain
fastening your door
to its plaintive frame.

We count night by a plateful
of spiders, and later we count day
by the spiders' shells.

We sing out each hour
through mouths full of gravel.

We slit the throat you call bedtime
and swill her pinkish bleed.

35

Do not pretend
that you don't like it
when we threaten you.

We see you
getting pheromone stink
under the collar

moaning baldly.

When we creak your step
when we crack your glass
when we tap tap tap

that is a bone
that is all we have
though we are

very shiny
and filled
with beetles.

We are made
entirely of bone.

Like an idol.
Like the tusk
of some wonderful past.

When you cleave to us
your skin will fuse
hot calcium meth

and in the myth
you will be named for us.

ACKNOWLEDGMENTS

Poems from *The Dead Girls Speak in Unison* first appeared in the Academy of American Poets *Poem-a-Day* project, *Barn Owl Review*, *Black Warrior Review*, *Black Warrior Review* National Poetry Month feature, *Delirious Hem*, *Dressing Room*, *Everyday Genius*, *Hick Poetics*, *Horse Less Press*, the *Huffington Post*, the *Kenyon Review*, the *Kenyon Review Online*, the *Nepotist*, *New Delta Review*, *New Delta Review*'s Best of the Web issue, *Pebble Lake Review*, *Rebellious Magazine*, *So to Speak*, *Spoon River Poetry Review*, and *Tarpaulin Sky*.

Excerpts appear as epigraphs in mystery novelist John Connolly's twelfth book in the Charlie Parker series, *Burning Soul*.

The poems borrow lines from Lucie Brock-Broido, Emily Dickinson, and Joni Mitchell.

ABOUT THE AUTHOR

Danielle Pafunda is the author of *The Dead Girls Speak in Unison* (Bloof Books, 2017), *Natural History Rape Museum* (Bloof Books, 2013), *Manhater* (Dusie Press, 2012), *Iatrogenic: Their Testimonies* (Noemi Press, 2010), *My Zorba* (Bloof Books, 2008), *Pretty Young Thing* (Soft Skull Press, 2005), and the chapbooks *Cram* (Essay Press, 2015) and *When You Left Me in the Rutted Terrain of Our Love at the Border, Which I Could Not Cross, Remaining a Citizen of this Corrupt Land* (Birds of Lace, 2014). Her poems have appeared in three editions of *The Best American Poetry* and have been anthologized in *Beauty is a Verb: The Poetics of Disability* (Cinco Puntos Press, 2011), *Gurlesque: The New Grrly, Grotesque, Burlesque Poetics* (Saturnalia Books, 2010), *Not for Mothers Only: Contemporary Poems on Child-Getting & Child Rearing* (Fence Books, 2007), *Hick Poetics* (Lost Roads Press, 2015), and *Please Excuse This Poem: 100 Poets for the Next Generation* (Penguin, 2015).

PRAISE FOR DANIELLE PAFUNDA

Danielle Pafunda abolishes the stereotype of prissy, dainty girls in her thrilling poetry collection *The Dead Girls Speak in Unison*. Set in a surrealistic underworld, takes on the collective voice of empowered female corpses and ironically uses quaint language and structure to describe the true nature of women. Pafunda's collection leaves readers craving more of its "rotten pages." —***Verse*, Brittany Capps**

We don't often see choral speakers, but speaking in unison gives these girls collective presence, forcing us to face gender violence. [T]he girls gain a certain power in this . . . raw girls who bypass maturity, who are as rank and offensive as possible. These unrefined girls are deeply unsettling. —***The Plot*, Heidi Czerwiec**

If you, like me, abhor under-forty Pulitzer Gang-Banged Glamor Balls guzzling down official verse-culture jizz, then join me in Danielle Pafunda's *Natural History Rape Museum*—no other book I know has so thoroughly shaken the fuckwad out of my pudenda, these violently subversive verses a lyrical tour de force. —***Coldfront*, Timothy Liu**

Danielle Pafunda's fifth book shows her at the top of her hilarious, furious game. One must reach for the oldest stories to describe the particular clawed, fanged, winged, and always female bodies of these texts. Pafunda's poetry is always a spiky sonic treat, punching a tracheostomy in the throat of lyric convention so that the noise of erased, extinguished, and strangled women can come out.

—***Poetry Project Newsletter*, Joyelle McSweeney**

Danielle Pafunda is at it again, thank goodness: saying what almost no one else will say, as only she can say it. Read her for the reality check; come back for the rhetorical rocket fuel. *Manhater* collects the language of the body, the body, the body. The world lurking in its pages "expels symmetry," surveys . . . the sunrise / barf," invites the "bitch seizure," will "shard and glisten" for you. Enter and "wait for the tremble." —**Evie Shockley**

Danielle Pafunda's *Iatrogenic* is that rare book for which we can never be ready. It is a fat valise of incendiary poems. Where has it come from? How should I know? Perhaps Lady Pafunda wrested this language from birds. In any case, she has infected me and recruited me with her "thick sting of pleasure." There is nothing extinct about her.

—**Rachel Zucker**

The outrageous love child of Berryman's squirrelly syntax and Dickinson's hermetic phrasal splicing, *My Zorba* envisions language as a peek-a-boo theater. Part oracle, part exhibitionist, the speaker of these missives wields her fractured "I" through the polysex costumage of gender. Pafunda's finger-in-the-eye pole dance sparkles with gothic fantasias created from the medical detritus of culturally annihilated bodies, dissected by the complicity of our own voyeuristic gaze.

—**Lara Glenum**

Her sexual and social frankness will remind you of the mid-period Anne Sexton, for like Sexton, Pafunda is rebelling against a system which has a name for everything except the things most important to a human, not to mention a woman. —**Kevin Killian**

www.ingramcontent.com/pod-product-compliance
Lightning Source LLC
Chambersburg PA
CBHW020950090426
42736CB00010B/1349